# THE BEST OF JOHN P. KEE

ISBN 978-1-4234-5713-8

HAL•LEONARD® CORPORATION

7777 W. BLUEMOUND RD. P.O. BOX 13819 MILWAUKEE, WI 53213

Visit Hal Leonard Online at
**www.halleonard.com**

# THE ANOINTING

Words and Music by
JOHN P. KEE

**Slowly, in 2**

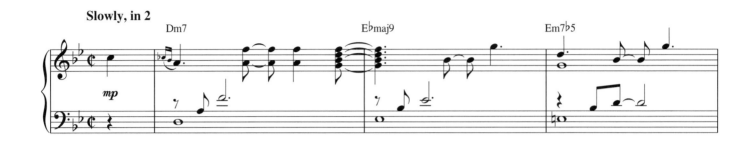

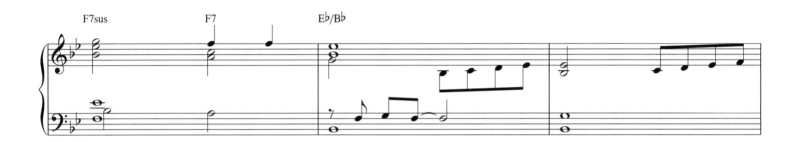

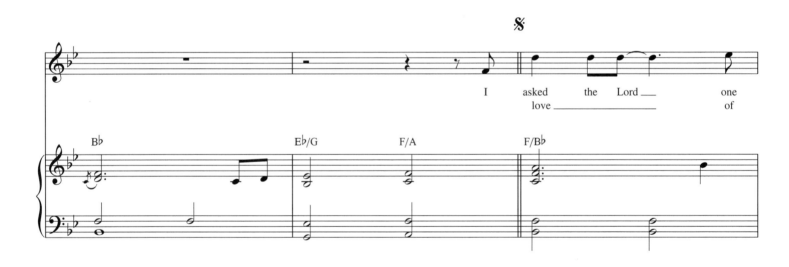

I asked the Lord ___ one
love ___ of

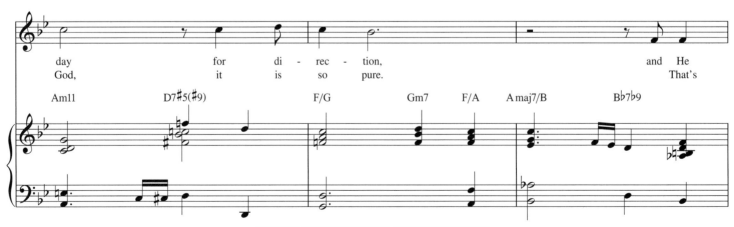

day for di - rec - tion,
God, it is so pure.

and He
That's

**To Coda** ⊕

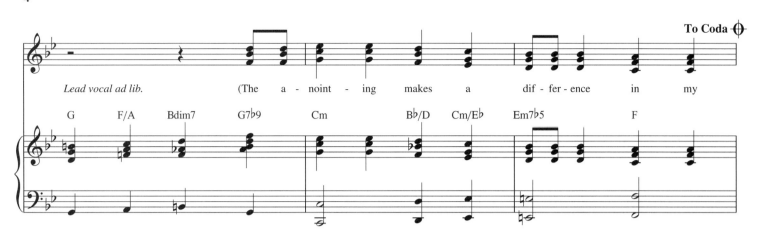

*Lead vocal ad lib.* (The a - noint - ing makes a dif - fer - ence in my

G    F/A    Bdim7    G7♭9    Cm    B♭/D    Cm/E♭    Em7♭5    F

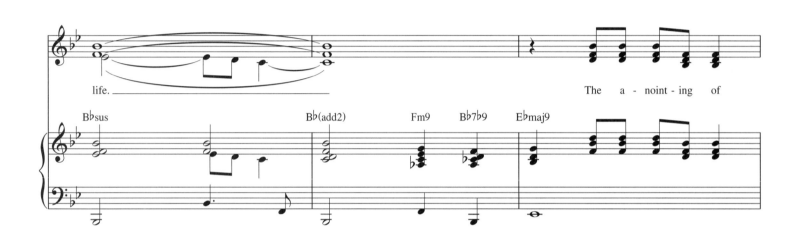

life. _____ The a - noint - ing of

B♭sus    B♭(add2)    Fm9    B♭7♭9    E♭maj9

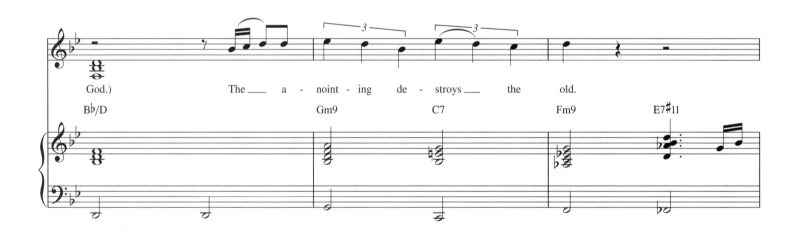

God.) The \_\_ a - noint - ing de - stroys \_\_ the old.

B♭/D    Gm9    C7    Fm9    E7#11

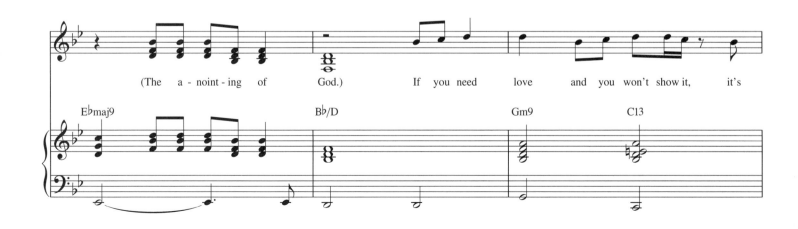

(The a - noint - ing of God.) If you need love and you won't show it, it's

E♭maj9    B♭/D    Gm9    C13

# I DO WORSHIP

Words and Music by
JOHN P. KEE

pres - ence.     We     will ___

A♭m7     D♭   G♭7♭9(♯11)   F7♯5     B♭m7     E♭m7

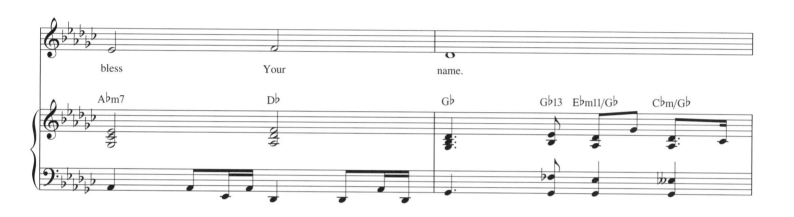

bless     Your     name.

A♭m7     D♭     G♭     G♭13  E♭m11/G♭  C♭m/G♭

For Your good - ness and ___ Your glo - ry,     for the

G♭(add2)  E♭m9  A♭7♯5     D♭m9     G♭13sus     G♭13♯11

joy in - side ___ Your sto - ry,     for the peace You gave ___ to me,

C♭maj9     E9   E♭m11  A♭7♯5     D♭m9

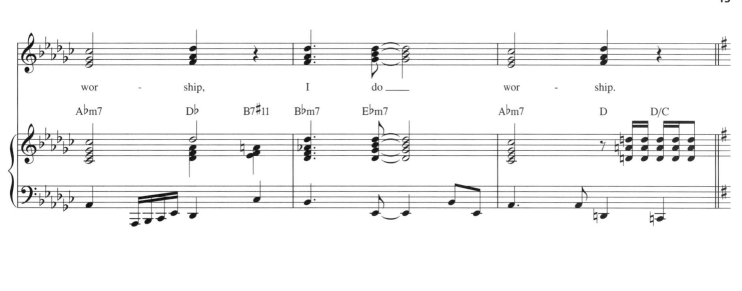

wor - ship, I do ____ wor - ship.

Abm7　　　Db　　B7#11　Bbm7　　Ebm7　　　　Abm7　　　D　　D/C

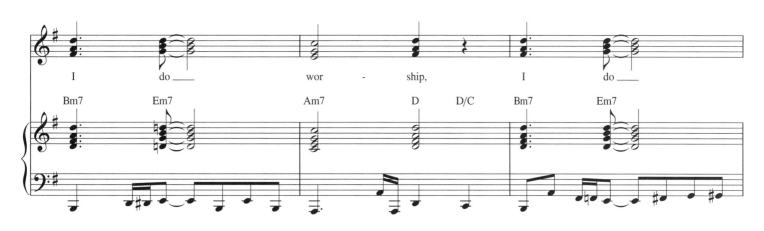

I　　do ____　　wor - ship,　　I　　do ____

Bm7　　　Em7　　　　　　Am7　　　D　　D/C　Bm7　　　Em7

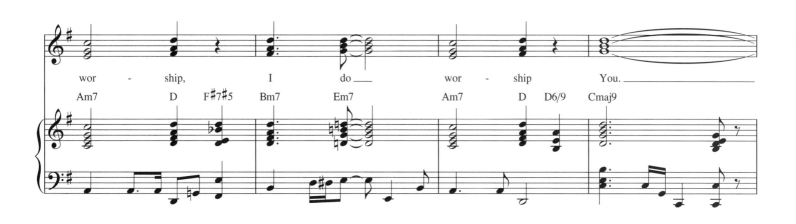

wor - ship,　　I　　do ____　wor - ship　You. ____

Am7　　　D　F#7#5　Bm7　　Em7　　　Am7　　D　D6/9　Cmaj9

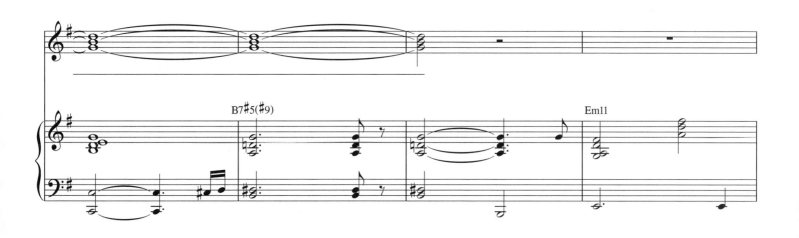

B7#5(#9)　　　　　　　　　　　　　　Em11

# GREATER

Words and Music by
JOHN P. KEE

# HE'LL WELCOME ME

Words and Music by
JOHN P. KEE

I'm liv-ing this life _____ just to live a - gain,
*(Lead vocal ad lib.)*

and with the Lord I know that I shall reign.

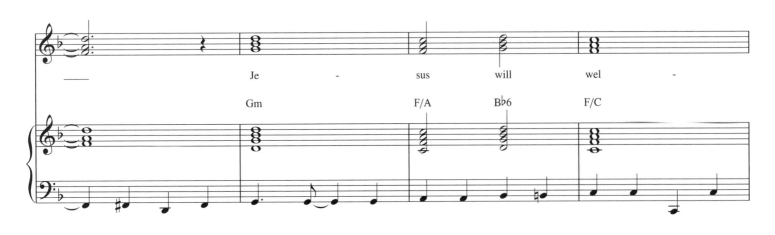

Je - sus will wel -

Gm    F/A    Bb6    F/C

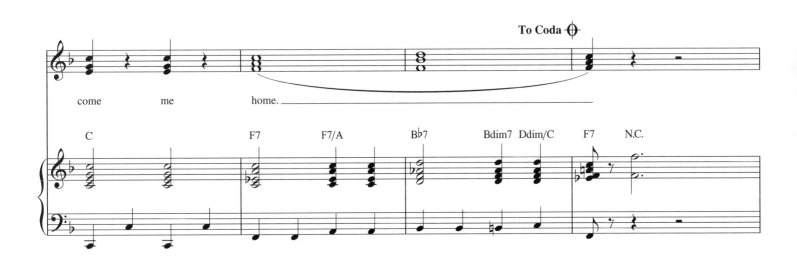

**To Coda** ⊕

come    me    home. _____

C    F7    F7/A    Bb7    Bdim7  Ddim/C    F7    N.C.

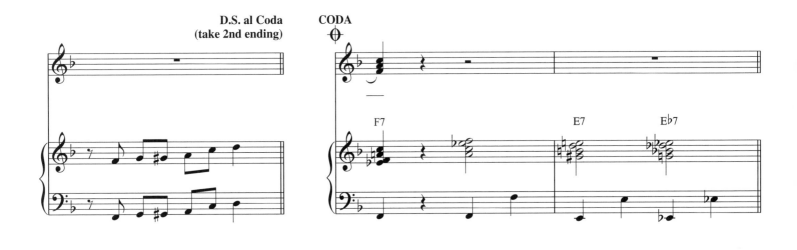

**D.S. al Coda**
**(take 2nd ending)**

**CODA** ⊕

F7    E7    Eb7

I _____ shall    see    Him    for _____ my -

D

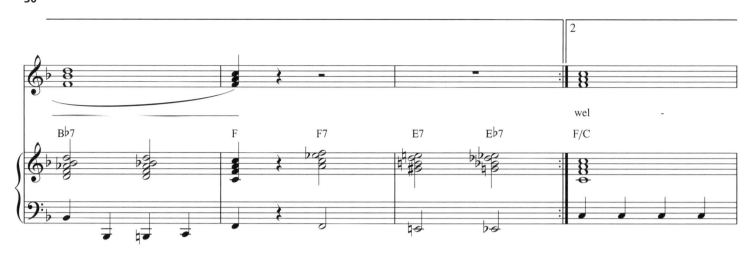

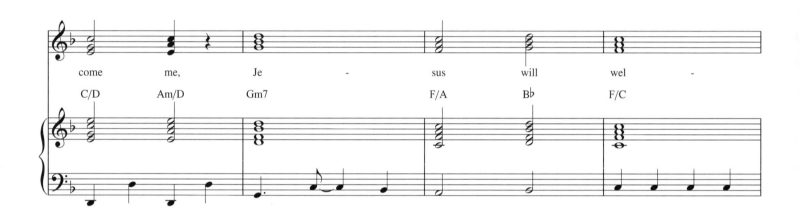

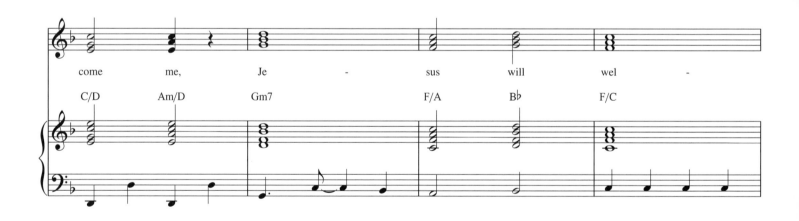

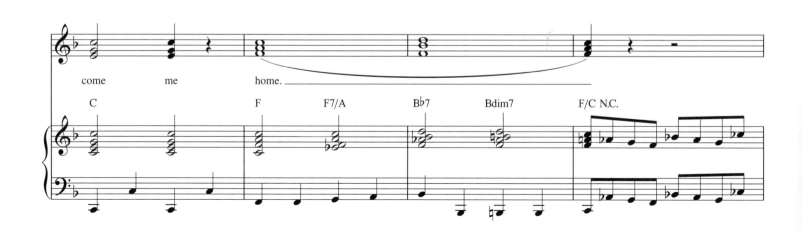

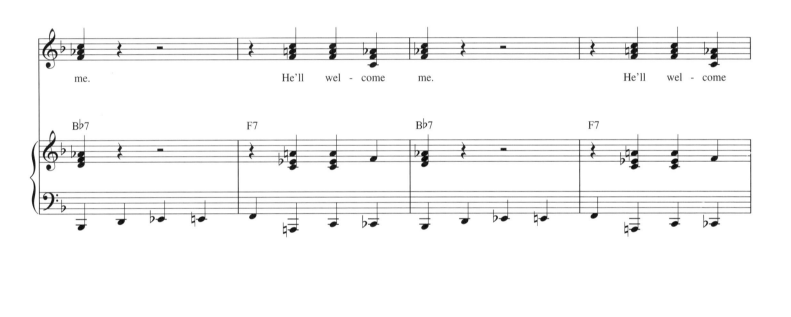

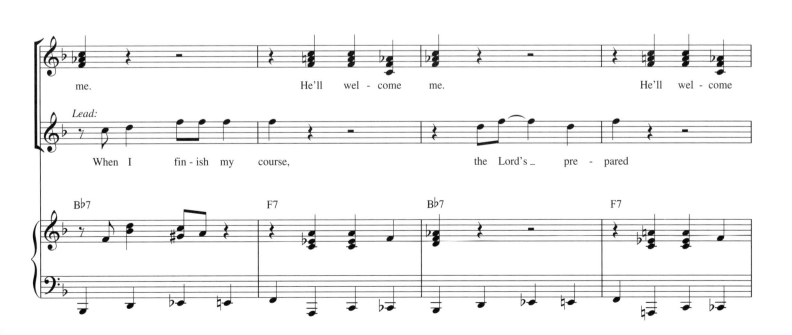

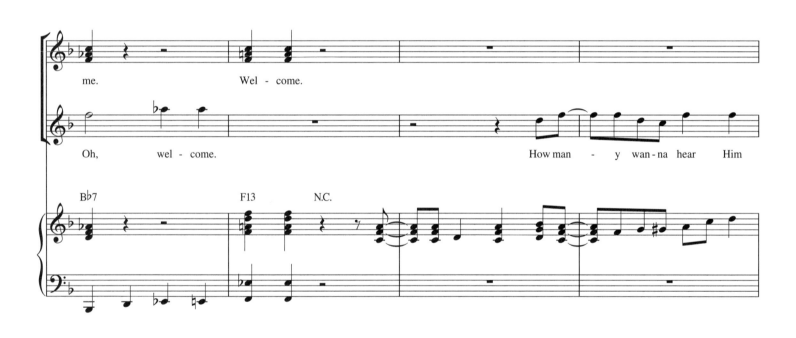

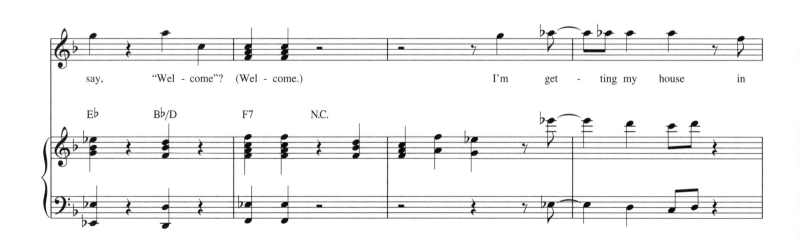

or - der to - day. (Wel - come home.) You've been faith - ful a - bout the

(Wel - come, My good and faith - ful ser -

few things. ___ That's what He's gon - na tell me.

- vant.) (He'll wel - come, yes, He'll wel - come, He'll wel - come,

When He called my name for e - ter - nal life.

34

yes, He'll wel-come me.) (He'll wel-come me.) (He'll wel-come

I'm wait-ing on church. Ah, just shake my _____ hand.

B♭7    F7    B♭7    F7

me.) (He'll wel-come me.) (He'll wel-come

I'm wait-ing on church. _____ With Him I'll stand. __

B♭7    F7    B♭7    F7

me.) (He'll wel-come me.) (He'll wel-come

Give me my robe; _ dressed it down in white.

B♭7    F7    B♭7    F7

# SOVEREIGN

Words and Music by
JOHN P. KEE

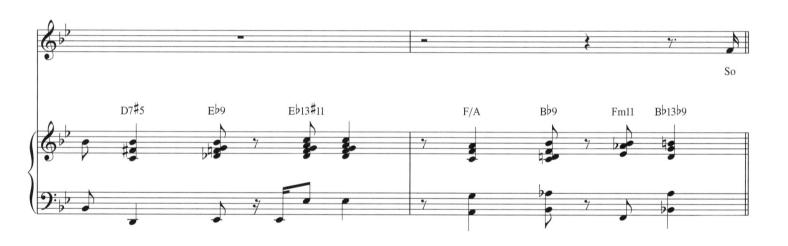

1st time only:
man - y things we __ don't know. Say it's hard to let go. We must

2nd time only:
ri - ah spoke __ of You. It was clear, it __ was true how per - so -

So

My God will do what He wants ___ to, ___ when-ev - er He wants ___

(My God will do what He wants ___ to, when-ev - er He wants

Bb/F    F/Eb    Bb7/D  Cm7  Bdim7    Cm7    Cm7b5  Bb/D Ebdim7 Bb/F

___ to. (He is God.) ___ *Women:* Sov - 'reign,

to. He is God.) ___ *Women:* Sov - 'reign,

F7    Bb(add2)

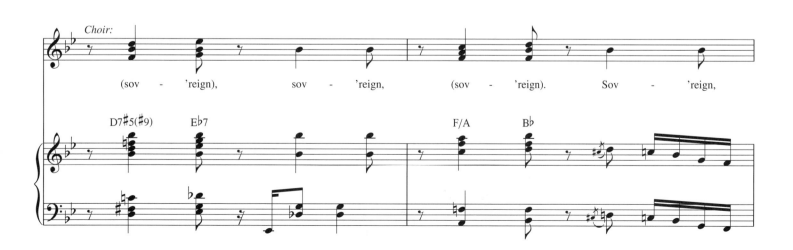

*Choir:*
(sov - 'reign), sov - 'reign, (sov - 'reign). Sov - 'reign,

D7#5(#9) Eb7    F/A    Bb

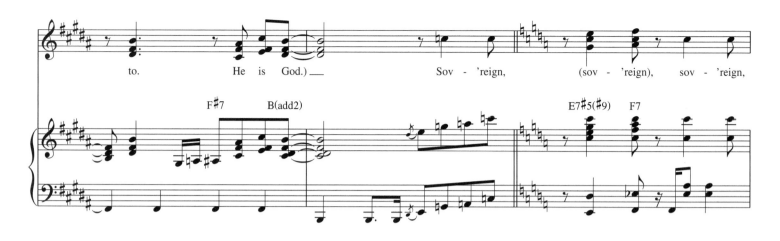

to.      He  is  God.) __      Sov - 'reign,      (sov - 'reign),      sov - 'reign,

F#7      B(add2)      E7#5(#9)      F7

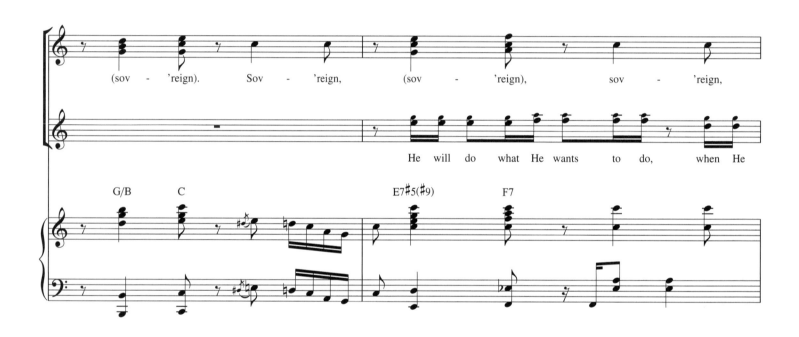

(sov - 'reign).      Sov - 'reign,      (sov - 'reign),      so - 'reign,

He  will  do  what  He  wants  to  do,      when  He

G/B      C      E7#5(#9)      F7

(sov - 'reign).      Sov - 'reign,      (sov - 'reign),      sov - 'reign,

gets  read - y  to  do ____  it.

G/B      C      E7#5(#9)      F7

# IN YOUR NAME

Words and Music by
JOHN P. KEE

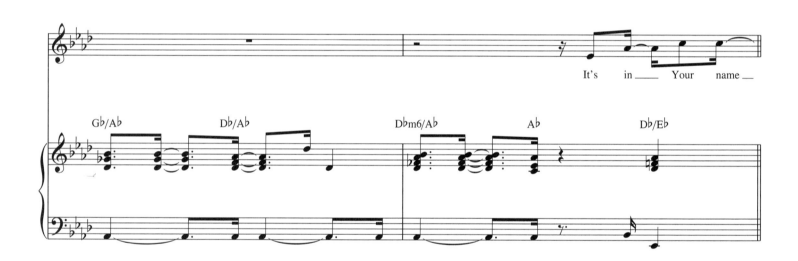

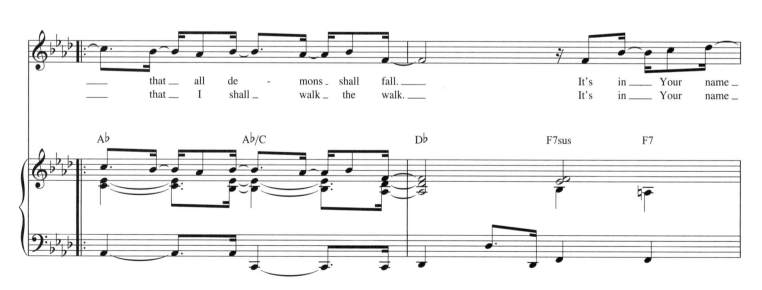

Lyrics:
It's in ___ Your name ___ ___ that ___ all de - mons shall fall. ___ It's in ___ Your name ___
___ that ___ I shall ___ walk ___ the walk. ___ It's in ___ Your name ___

in \_\_\_ Your name. \_\_\_\_\_

Ooh, _____

Ab/Bb    Eb/Bb

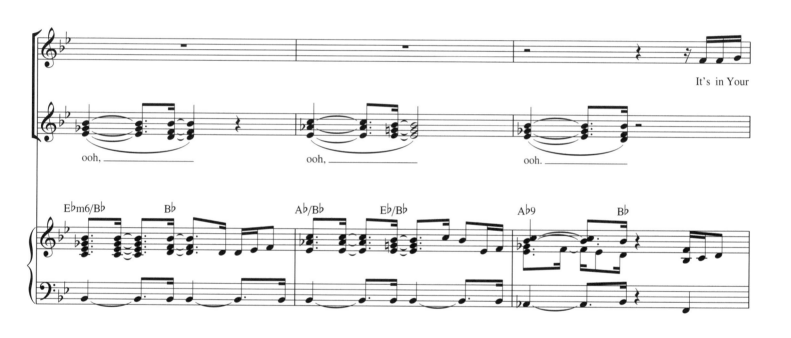

It's in Your

ooh, _____    ooh, _____    ooh. _____

Ebm6/Bb    Bb    Ab/Bb    Eb/Bb    Ab9    Bb

name \_\_\_\_\_ we wor - ship,    it's in Your name \_\_\_\_\_ we praise. \_ *(Lead vocal ad lib. to end)*

It's in Your

Ab/Bb    Eb/Bb    Ebm6/Bb    Bb

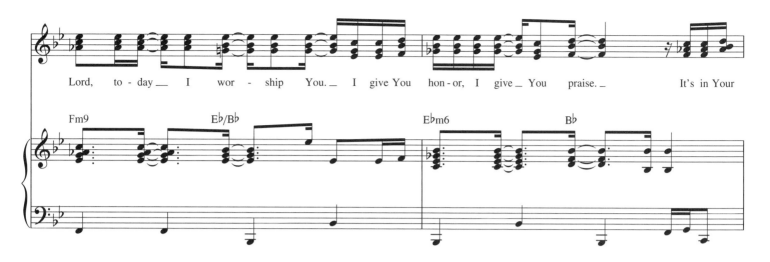

Lord, to-day __ I wor-ship You. __ I give You hon-or, I give __ You praise. __ It's in Your

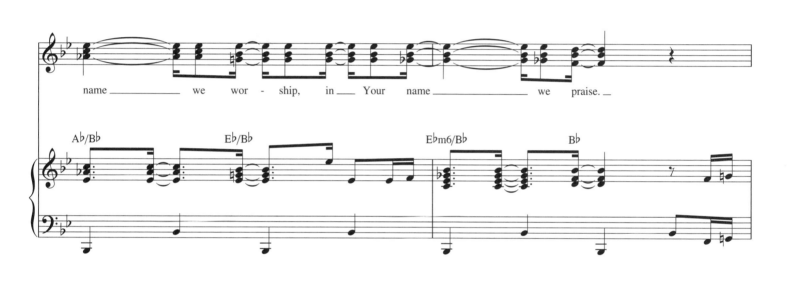

name _____ we wor - ship, in __ Your name _____ we praise. __ It's in Your

# JESUS IS REAL

Words and Music by
JOHN KEE

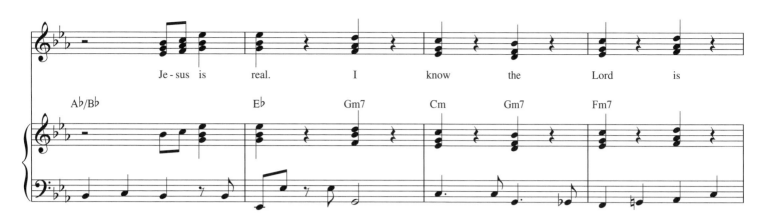

Je - sus is real. I know the Lord is

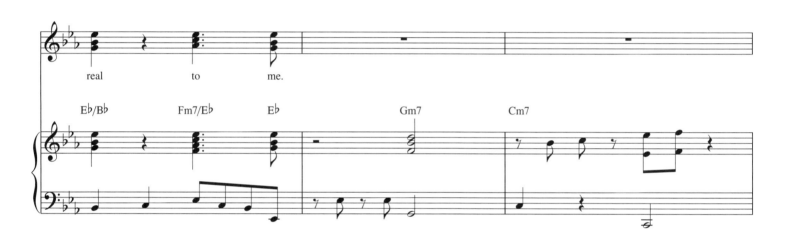

real to me.

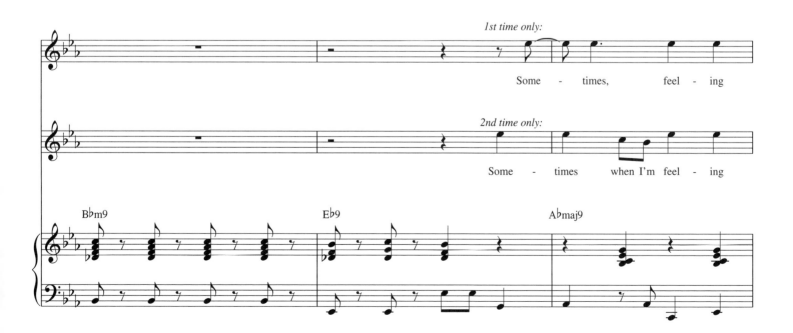

*1st time only:*

Some - times, feel - ing

*2nd time only:*

Some - times when I'm feel - ing

low,          and no - where   to   go,

down,          no one     a - round,

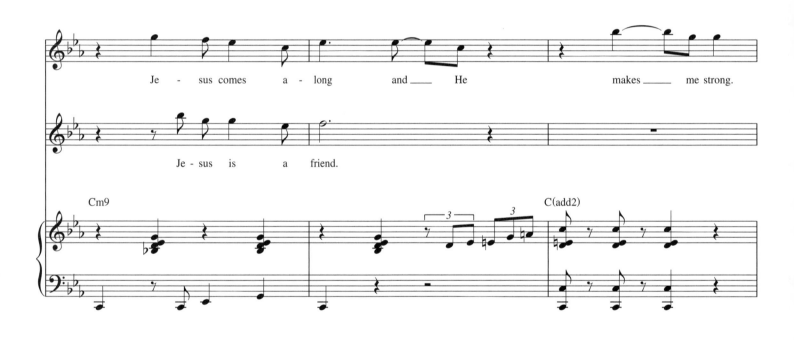

Je - sus comes a - long   and    He        makes    me strong.

Je - sus is a friend.

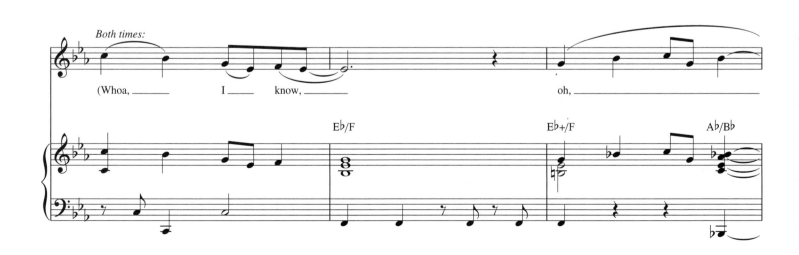

*Both times:*

(Whoa,     I    know,            oh,

I _____ know ___ that ___ the Lord ___ will ___ take good care of

I can e-ven feel Him ___ from the crown ___ of my head ___ to my toes.

Cm9

C(add2)

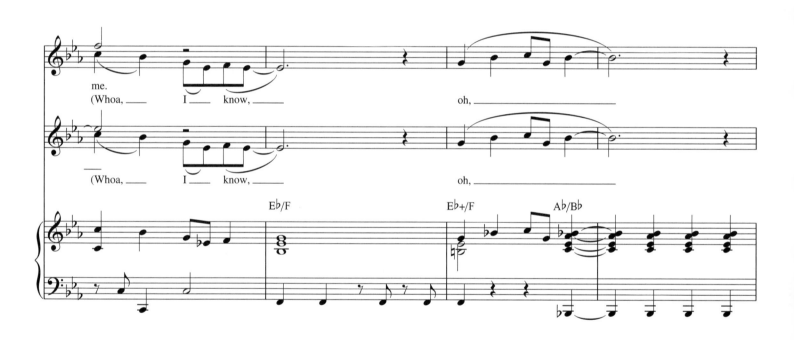

me.
(Whoa, ___ I ___ know, _____ oh, _____

(Whoa, ___ I ___ know, _____ oh, _____

Eb/F

Eb+/F

Ab/Bb

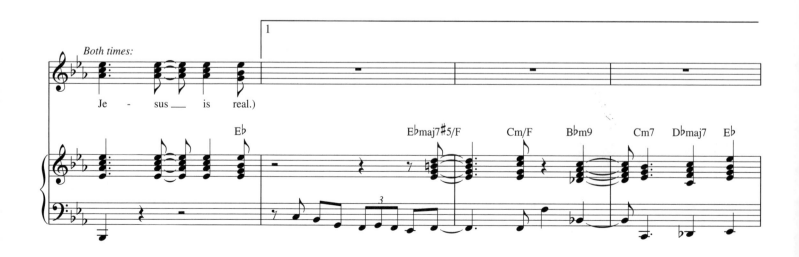

*Both times:*

Je - sus ___ is real.)

Eb

Ebmaj7#5/F  Cm/F  Bbm9  Cm7  Dbmaj7  Eb

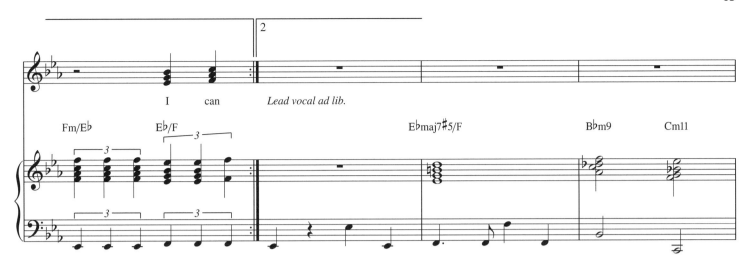

I can *Lead vocal ad lib.*

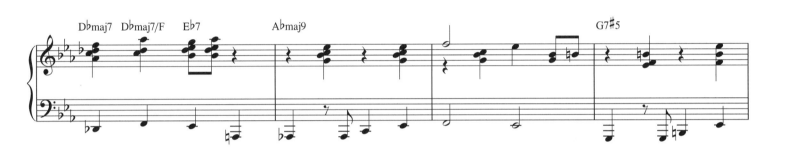

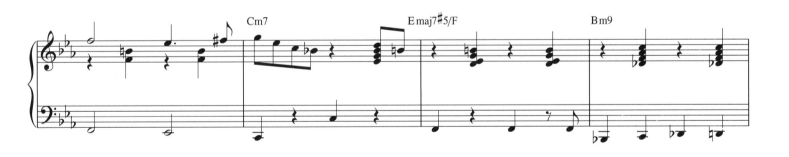

Real!
yeah!

(Real!)
(Yeah!)

Real!
Yeah!

# MIGHTY GOD

Words and Music by
JOHN P. KEE

* Recorded a half step lower.

# MY MIND IS MADE UP

Words and Music by
JOHN P. KEE

Moderately fast, in 2

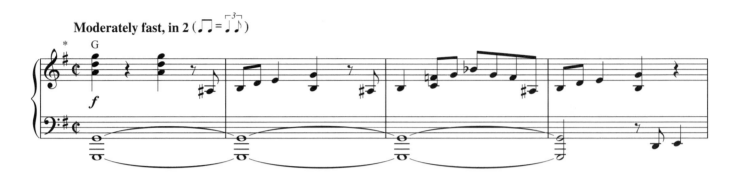

Since I met the Lord, my mind is made up, (My mind is made up.)

to go with Je - sus all the way. (All the way.)

*Recorded a half step lower.*

(I'm on the right track; there's no turn - ing back.)

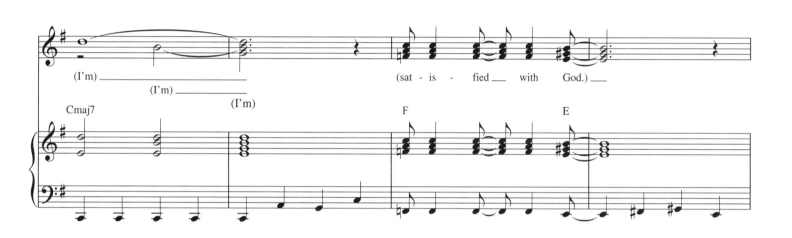

(I'm) _____ (I'm) _____ (I'm) _____ (sat - is - fied __ with God.) __

(No - bod - y can hold me, no - bod - y can mold me,

**To Coda**

no - bod - y can show me like You, Je - sus.)

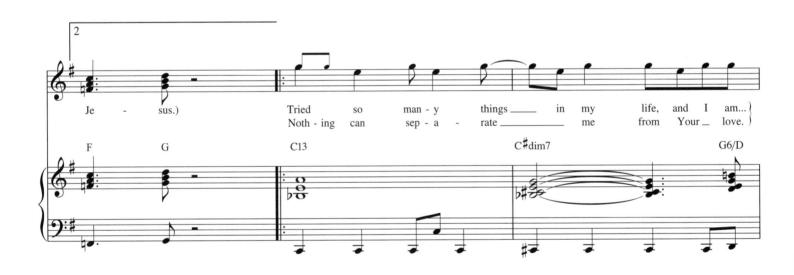

Je - sus.) Tried so man - y things ____ in my life, and I am...
Noth - ing can sep - a - rate _____ me from Your __ love.

(I am __ so sat - is - fied.) __ I'll nev - er turn __ my back __
Re - newed __ my joy _____ like __

# SHOW UP!

Words and Music by
JOHN KEE

never give in. ___ On-ly the strong shall sur-vive ___ and win.

never give in. ___ On-ly the strong, ___ shall sur-vive ___ and win.

(1., 2.) Just ask the ques-tion, and the an-swer shall come. Just ex-er-cise your faith, and

know He's the One. If there is no sign, ___ keep this in mind: ___ He'll show ___

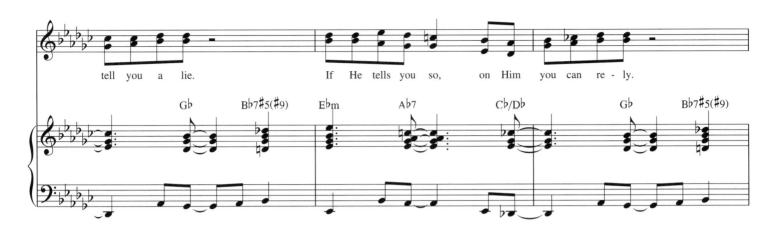

tell you a lie.      If He tells you so,     on Him you can re-ly.

God is not a man    that will tell you a lie.        If He tells you so,    on Him

*Men:* God is not a man...      tell you a lie.        If He tells you so...

you can re-ly.    *Choir:* If there is no sign, ___        if

you can re-ly.

**Play 3 times**

Show up!

Show up!

**Play 4 times**

Show up!

Show up!

Show up!

Show up!

# STRENGTH

Words and Music by
JOHN P. KEE

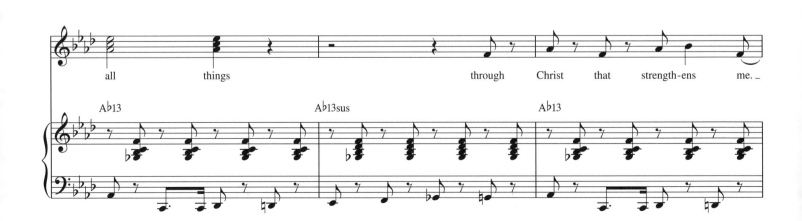

# WASH ME

Words and Music by
JOHN P. KEE

* Recorded a half step lower.

# WE GLORIFY

Words and Music by
JOHN P. KEE

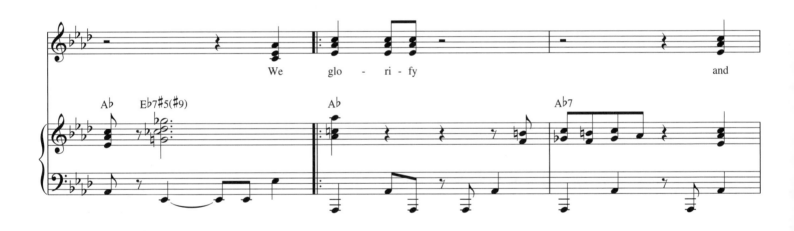

We glo - ri - fy and

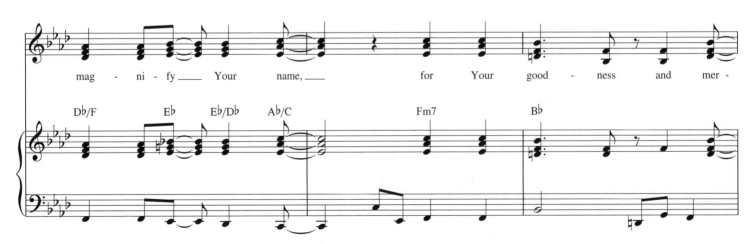

mag - ni - fy___ Your name, ___ for Your good - ness and mer -

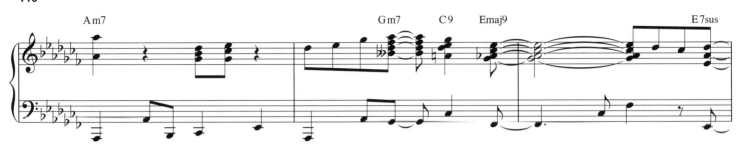

We praise and

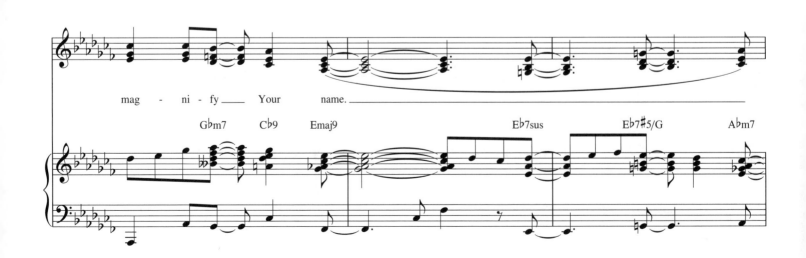

mag - ni - fy___ Your name. ___

We praise and mag - ni - fy___ Your name.___

G♭m7    C♭9    Emaj13

E♭/B♭

E♭7    A♭m    N.C.

B 7sus    D/C    D 9    Ddim7

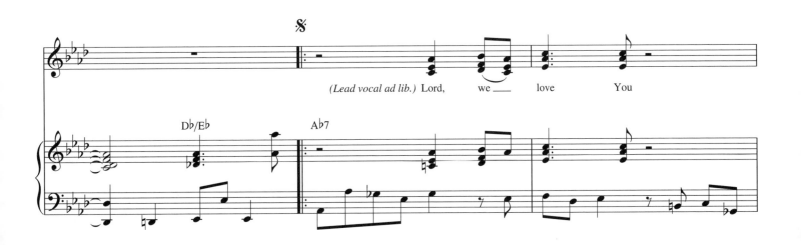

*(Lead vocal ad lib.)* Lord,    we___ love    You

D♭/E♭

A♭7

# THANK YOU, LORD
## (He Did It All)

Words and Music by
JOHN P. KEE

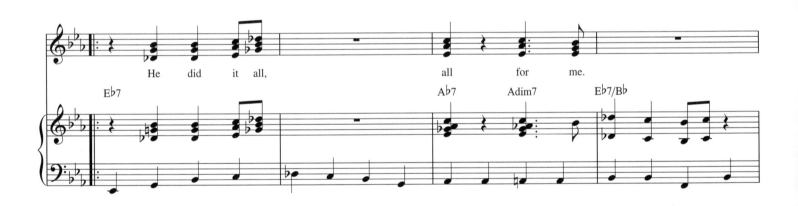

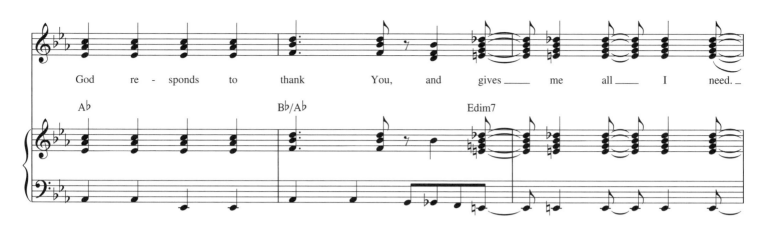

God re - sponds to thank You, and gives \_\_\_ me all \_\_\_ I need. \_\_

He did it all _____ for \_\_\_ me. _____

You did it all _____
He did it all _____ when

back on Cal - va - ry.  That's \_\_ why I \_\_ be - lieve \_\_
I thanked Him \_\_ in ad - vance.  While \_\_ oth - ers cry and com - plain, \_\_

119